EMPOWERMENT ABC:

A Journey of Resilience for People with Disabilities

Alexis Jose Cabauatan

Copyright

Empowerment ABC: A Journey of Resilience for People with Disabilities

1st edition

By Alexis Jose Cabauatan

September 2023

Published by:
Alexis Jose Cabauatan
+63918 398 7461
Manla, Philippines
phscriber@gmail.com

ISBN: 978-621-06-0964-6

Dedication

To all the incredible individuals with disabilities,

This book is dedicated to you—for your unwavering strength, boundless courage, and relentless determination. Each chapter of this book reflects the incredible journey you've embarked upon, filled with challenges, triumphs, and a spirit that knows no bounds.

May these words be a source of inspiration, a reminder of your innate power, and a testament to the remarkable impact you make on the world. Your journey of empowerment is a beacon of hope, a testament to the human spirit's resilience, and a catalyst for positive change.

As you navigate life's twists and turns, may you always remember that you are not defined by your limitations, but rather by your boundless potential. Your voices, your stories, and your advocacy are shaping a world that values inclusivity, celebrates diversity, and fosters understanding.

With deep admiration and utmost respect,

Alexis JC

Table of Contents

Copyright....2
Dedication....3
Introduction....6
Acceptance....8
Belief....11
Communication....14
Determination....17
Empathy....19
Flexibility....22
Gratitude....25
Hope....28
Independence....31
Joy....34
Knowledge....37
Love....40
Mindfulness....43

Never Giving Up....46

Overcoming Challenges....49

Perseverance....52

Quality of Life....55

Resilience....58

Self-Advocacy....61

Transformation....64

Understanding....67

Vision....70

Wellness....73

Xenodochia....76

Yearning for Change....79

Zeal for Life....82

Epilogue: A Journey of Empowerment....85

Acknowledgments:....87

About the Book:....89

About the Author:....91

Introduction

In a world where challenges often seem insurmountable, there exists a remarkable community of individuals who have turned adversity into a journey of empowerment. "Empowerment ABC: A Journey of Resilience for People with Disabilities" is not just a book—it's an immersive experience designed to inspire, empower, and guide you through your own path of personal growth and transformation. Within these pages, you'll embark on an inspiring voyage through the alphabet, where each letter represents a pivotal aspect of living life to the fullest despite disabilities.

Imagine a world where acceptance is not just a word, but a powerful tool that transforms obstacles into stepping stones. Picture a realm where self-belief is an unshakable foundation upon which dreams are built. Envision a place where communication bridges the gaps between hearts and minds, creating connections that uplift and inspire. This book invites you to enter that world, to explore the depths of empathy, to soar on the wings of hope, and to walk hand-in-hand with resilience.

But this journey is not a solitary one—it's an interactive exploration that invites you to reflect, engage, and participate actively. Throughout the chapters, you'll find spaces for reflection, writing prompts, and activities that encourage you to delve deeper into the concepts presented. These moments of pause are your opportunities to connect with the material on a personal level, applying it to your own experiences, and forging a more profound connection with your own journey.

From A for Acceptance to Z for Zeal, the chapters in this book are a celebration of the human spirit's indomitable drive to rise above limitations. As you read, you'll encounter stories of individuals who have harnessed their inner strength to overcome adversity. You'll also find insights from experts who provide practical steps towards empowerment and personal growth. However, it doesn't stop there—throughout the book, you'll be encouraged to jot down your thoughts, feelings, and ideas in the provided journal sections. These journal entries become your personal record of growth and progress, capturing the unique essence of your journey.

But this book is not just about reflection; it's also about action. The activities peppered throughout the chapters invite you to apply the concepts to your life in tangible ways. Whether it's setting goals, practicing self-compassion, or creating a vision board, these activities empower you to take the ideas off the pages and into your everyday life.

In the spirit of unity, let us set sail on this participatory journey together. The challenges and triumphs you'll experience are not only shared by countless others but also an essential part of what makes you who you are. "Empowerment ABC: A Journey of Resilience for People with Disabilities" is more than a book—it's a tool, a companion, and a source of inspiration. So, let us embark on this transformative odyssey, one reflection, one journal entry, and one activity at a time. As we do so, we illuminate the path toward a brighter, more inclusive future—together.

Acceptance

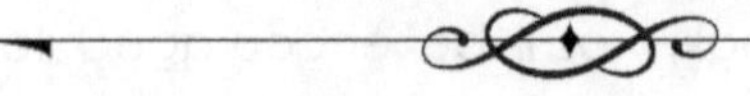

Acceptance was a turning point for me, it allowed me to redirect my energy from fighting against my disability to working with it. I began exploring adaptive technologies, which eventually led to newfound passions and opportunities.

Acceptance isn't a one-time event; it's a dynamic process that unfolds over time. It involves acknowledging both the challenges and the possibilities that come with a disability. Acceptance doesn't mean surrendering to limitations; rather, it's a strategic decision to acknowledge the situation as it is and then explore how to make the most of it. Through acceptance, you can reclaim your power, shed the weight of denial or self-blame, and redirect your energy towards meaningful pursuits.

Acceptance involves cultivating self-compassion and reframing your self-talk. Instead of viewing your disability as a hindrance, consider it as a unique aspect of your identity—one that adds depth to your life story. Acceptance empowers you to take charge of your narrative, embracing your journey with all its triumphs and challenges.

Acceptance is not a linear path. It's okay to have moments of frustration or sadness. Acceptance doesn't mean ignoring these emotions; it means allowing yourself to feel them while also recognizing your capacity to grow and adapt.

Reflection:

Reflect on your own journey of acceptance. What were the initial challenges you faced in coming to terms with your disability? How have your perceptions evolved over time? Consider moments that marked your transition from resistance to embracing your circumstances. Write down these moments and reflect on how they have shaped your outlook.

Journal Entry:

In your journal, write a letter to yourself, addressing the progress you've made in accepting your disability. Reflect on the positive changes acceptance has brought to your life. Write about any new experiences, friendships, or opportunities that have emerged as a result of embracing your reality. Don't hesitate to share words of encouragement for your future self on this ongoing journey.

____

Activity:

Create a visual representation of acceptance through art or collage. Use colors, shapes, and symbols to depict the transformation from resistance to embracing your reality. Include elements that represent your personal growth and the strength you've discovered within yourself. This visual representation can serve as a powerful reminder of your journey and the resilience you embody.

Belief

Believing in myself was the first step towards becoming a competitive athlete, I learned that my limitations didn't define me. Instead, my determination and hard work propelled me forward.

Belief is the cornerstone upon which empowerment is built. It's the unshakable foundation that propels individuals with disabilities to surpass expectations and achieve greatness. Self-belief is not about arrogance; it's a steadfast confidence in your inherent worth and potential. By cultivating self-belief, you're harnessing the power to shape your own destiny and define success on your terms.

Believing in yourself involves recognizing your strengths and accomplishments, no matter how small they may seem. It's about quieting the inner critic and embracing a self-compassionate mindset. When you believe in your abilities, you're more likely to tackle challenges head-on, push through adversity, and find innovative solutions. Your self-belief becomes a source of motivation, fueling your determination to overcome obstacles.

The transformative impact of self-belief. Our beliefs shape our reality. When individuals with disabilities believe in their potential, they open doors to possibilities that might have otherwise remained closed.

Reflection:

Reflect on instances in your life where your self-belief has led to positive outcomes. How has believing in yourself allowed you to overcome challenges? Think about moments when self-doubt held you back and how shifting your mindset could have changed the outcome. Write down your reflections to remind yourself of the power of self-belief.

Journal Entry:

Write about a time when you surprised yourself by achieving something you initially thought was beyond your capabilities. How did your self-belief contribute to that achievement? Reflect on how you can continue to nurture and strengthen your self-belief moving forward.

____

____

____

____

____

____

____

____

____

____

____

____

____

____

____

____

Activity:

Create a "Self-Belief Jar." Decorate a jar and fill it with small notes of accomplishments, compliments, and affirmations. Whenever you need a boost of self-belief, reach into the jar and read a note. This tangible reminder of your worth and capabilities can help reinforce your belief in yourself.

Communication

When we communicate our stories and challenges, we're breaking down barriers and fostering understanding, our stories humanize our experiences and build bridges of empathy.

Communication is the bridge that connects hearts, minds, and experiences. For individuals with disabilities, effective communication is a powerful tool that not only allows them to express their needs but also fosters understanding and connection with others. Communication goes beyond words—it encompasses body language, gestures, and even the unspoken emotions that tie us together.

Effective communication begins with self-awareness. By understanding your own thoughts, emotions, and needs, you can better convey them to others. It's also essential to cultivate active listening skills, showing respect for others' perspectives and experiences. When you communicate with openness and empathy, you invite others to do the same, creating an environment of mutual respect and understanding.

Effective communication allows individuals with disabilities to advocate for themselves and their needs, it's a way of asserting their voice and ensuring their preferences are heard and respected.

Reflection:

Reflect on moments when effective communication has made a positive impact in your life. Consider times when misunderstandings were resolved through open dialogue. How did these experiences shape your connections with others? Write down your reflections to remind yourself of the value of effective communication.

Journal Entry:

Write about a situation where effective communication helped you advocate for yourself or share your perspective. How did you approach the conversation? Reflect on what you learned from that experience and how you can continue to improve your communication skills.

____

____

____

____

____

____

____

____

____

____

____

____

____

____

____

____

Activity:

Engage in a role-playing activity where you practice assertive communication. Choose a scenario where you need to express your needs or preferences. Practice using clear, respectful language while also actively listening to the other person's responses. Reflect on the experience and consider how you can apply these communication skills in real-life situations.

Determination

I faced countless rejections in my artistic career, But I refused to give up. Every 'no' only fueled my determination to prove that my disability didn't define my abilities.

Determination is the fuel that drives individuals with disabilities to overcome challenges, both big and small. It's the unwavering commitment to pursuing goals, even in the face of adversity. Determination goes hand in hand with resilience, allowing you to bounce back from setbacks and continue moving forward with purpose.

Determination involves setting clear goals and breaking them down into manageable steps. It's about cultivating a growth mindset that views obstacles as opportunities for growth and learning. When you approach challenges with determination, you're not just striving to succeed; you're building the strength to withstand future challenges with greater resilience.

Determination propels individuals with disabilities to become the architects of their own success, it empowers them to transform obstacles into stepping stones.

Reflection:

Reflect on a time when your determination helped you overcome a significant challenge. What strategies or mindset shifts did you employ to push through? How did the experience shape your confidence and outlook on future challenges? Write down your reflections to remind yourself of your inner strength.

Journal Entry:

Write about a goal you're currently working towards. How can you channel your determination to make progress? Break down the steps you need to take and consider potential obstacles. Reflect on how your determination can guide you through each phase of your journey.

Activity:

Create a vision board that represents your determined pursuit of goals. Collect images, words, and symbols that symbolize your aspirations. Display the vision board in a place where you'll see it daily, allowing it to serve as a visual reminder of your determination and the future you're working towards.

Empathy

By sharing my own stories and challenges, I've seen how empathy can shift perspectives, it's not just about sympathy; it's about genuinely connecting with others and acknowledging our shared humanity.

Empathy is the bridge that connects hearts, allowing us to understand and share the feelings of others. For individuals with disabilities, empathy is a powerful tool for building connections and breaking down barriers. It's about recognizing the humanity in each person and cultivating a compassionate understanding of their experiences.

Empathy begins with self-empathy—showing yourself the same compassion you extend to others. It's important to acknowledge your own feelings, struggles, and triumphs. This self-awareness forms the foundation for empathizing with others, allowing you to listen actively, acknowledge their experiences, and offer support without judgment.

Empathy has the remarkable ability to foster inclusivity and create a more understanding world. By embracing empathy, individuals with disabilities can advocate for themselves and contribute to positive change on a broader scale.

Empathy builds bridges of connection, when individuals with disabilities share their experiences, they educate others and pave the way for greater understanding and acceptance.

Reflection:

Reflect on a moment when someone showed empathy towards you. How did it make you feel? Consider times when empathy played a role in fostering understanding or resolving conflicts. Write down your reflections to remind yourself of the transformative power of empathy.

Journal Entry:

Write about a time when you practiced empathy towards someone else. How did you approach the situation? Reflect on how your empathy contributed to the connection between you and the other person. Consider how you can continue to cultivate empathy in your interactions.

Activity:

Engage in an empathy-building exercise. Choose a person you interact with regularly and set the intention to actively listen to their experiences. Ask open-ended questions and listen without judgment. Reflect on how this exercise deepened your understanding of the other person and strengthened your connection.

Flexibility

Adaptability wasn't always easy for me, but by embracing flexibility, I've discovered strengths and talents I didn't know I had. Every challenge became an opportunity for me to show just how resilient I am.

Flexibility is the art of adaptability—the ability to navigate life's twists and turns with grace and resilience. For individuals with disabilities, flexibility is a valuable skill that helps them respond effectively to changing circumstances. It involves embracing change, finding creative solutions, and maintaining a positive outlook even when faced with unexpected challenges.

Flexibility isn't about compromising your values or giving up on your goals; it's about approaching situations with an open mind and a willingness to adjust your approach. By cultivating flexibility, individuals with disabilities can transform obstacles into opportunities, demonstrating their capacity to thrive in diverse and dynamic environments.

Flexibility also involves learning from experience. Each new situation presents a chance to learn, grow, and refine your strategies. Through flexibility, you develop the capacity to navigate life's uncertainties and emerge stronger on the other side.

Flexibility allows individuals with disabilities to rewrite their narratives, it empowers them to find innovative solutions and embrace change as a catalyst for growth.

Reflection:

Reflect on a time when you demonstrated flexibility in the face of a challenge. How did your ability to adapt impact the outcome? Consider how your mindset and approach to the situation contributed to your success. Write down your reflections to remind yourself of the power of flexibility.

Journal Entry:

Write about a recent situation where you encountered unexpected changes. How did you respond? Reflect on what you learned from that experience and how it contributed to your personal growth. Consider how you can apply the lessons of flexibility to future situations.

____

Activity:

Engage in a problem-solving activity that requires flexibility. Choose a scenario that requires you to adjust your approach and find creative solutions. As you work through the challenge, reflect on the strategies you're using to adapt and the skills you're developing along the way.

Gratitude

Acknowledging the positives in my life has been transformative, it's not about ignoring challenges, but about finding reasons to smile and celebrating the victories, no matter how small.

Gratitude is a powerful practice that shifts our focus from what we lack to what we have. For individuals with disabilities, cultivating gratitude can be a transformative tool for enhancing well-being and fostering a positive outlook on life. It's about recognizing the blessings, both big and small, that enrich our experiences and bring joy to our days.

Gratitude is a way of acknowledging the progress you've made and the achievements you've accomplished. It's not about denying challenges but rather about finding silver linings and reasons to celebrate amidst the difficulties. By cultivating gratitude, individuals with disabilities can nurture a sense of contentment and resilience in the face of adversity.

Practicing gratitude also extends to recognizing the support and kindness of others. By acknowledging the efforts of caregivers, friends, and allies, individuals with disabilities can strengthen their support networks and build a sense of community.

Gratitude is a powerful antidote to negativity, by focusing on what we're thankful for, we shift our perspective and cultivate a more optimistic outlook.

Reflection:

Reflect on moments in your life when practicing gratitude has brought you joy. How did acknowledging the positives impact your mood and outlook? Consider how gratitude has helped you navigate challenges with a more resilient mindset. Write down your reflections to remind yourself of the power of gratitude.

Journal Entry:

Write a gratitude list, detailing three things you're grateful for today. These could be experiences, people, accomplishments, or even moments of self-discovery. Reflect on how acknowledging these positives enhances your overall well-being and sense of empowerment.

Activity:

Create a gratitude journal. Dedicate a notebook to recording daily moments of gratitude. Each day, jot down at least three things you're thankful for. Over time, you'll build a collection of positive experiences that serve as a reminder of the richness of your life.

Hope

In the face of adversity, hope became my lifeline, it allowed me to envision a future beyond my circumstances and fueled my determination to make it a reality.

Hope is the beacon that guides us through the darkest of times, reminding us that even in adversity, there's a light at the end of the tunnel. For individuals with disabilities, hope is a powerful source of motivation, resilience, and the belief in a better tomorrow. It's the unwavering belief that challenges can be overcome and dreams can be realized.

Hope involves envisioning a future filled with possibilities and setting goals that inspire you. It's about embracing optimism and maintaining a positive outlook, even when faced with setbacks. By cultivating hope, individuals with disabilities can tap into a wellspring of inner strength that empowers them to persevere through challenges.

Hope isn't a passive sentiment; it's an active force that propels you forward, urging you to take steps towards your aspirations. It's a reminder that with every challenge you conquer, you're inching closer to the future you've envisioned.

Hope is a powerful driver of action, Individuals with disabilities who cultivate hope are more likely to take proactive steps towards their goals and overcome obstacles.

Reflection:

Reflect on a time when hope guided you through a challenging situation. How did maintaining hope influence your mindset and actions? Consider how your sense of hope has evolved over time and the impact it has had on your resilience. Write down your reflections to remind yourself of the transformative power of hope.

Journal Entry:

Write about a dream or goal that you're hopeful about. How does envisioning this future inspire you to take action? Reflect on the steps you've already taken towards this goal and how each small victory brings you closer to its realization.

____
____
____
____
____
____
____
____
____
____
____
____
____
____
____
____

Activity:

Create a vision board that represents your hopeful future. Use images, quotes, and symbols that capture the essence of your aspirations. Display the vision board in a place where you'll see it daily, allowing it to serve as a visual reminder of the hope that propels you forward.

Independence

I've learned that asking for help is a sign of strength, not weakness. By embracing my support network, I've achieved goals that were once beyond my reach.

Independence is the ability to navigate life with self-sufficiency and autonomy while also recognizing when to seek support. For individuals with disabilities, independence takes on a unique meaning—it's about making choices that align with personal values and goals while embracing the support systems that enable success.

Independence doesn't mean doing everything alone; it means knowing when and how to ask for help. It involves advocating for your needs, setting boundaries, and actively participating in decisions that affect your life. By cultivating independence, individuals with disabilities can shape their own narratives and contribute to the broader community.

Independence also extends beyond physical capabilities—it includes emotional and psychological aspects. It's about developing the resilience to manage challenges and the confidence to chart your own path, embracing both triumphs and setbacks along the way.

Independence isn't about rejecting assistance, it's about knowing when and how to seek help, maintaining a sense of agency, and actively participating in decisions.

Reflection:

Reflect on a situation where you asserted your independence by making a choice aligned with your values. How did this decision empower you and contribute to your overall well-being? Consider how your understanding of independence has evolved over time. Write down your reflections to remind yourself of the complexity and significance of independence.

Journal Entry:

Write about a goal you're working towards that embodies your quest for independence. How are you actively participating in the process of achieving this goal? Reflect on how balancing autonomy and support has contributed to your progress. Consider the emotions and insights that arise from this reflection.

Activity:

Create a list of three ways you can assert your independence in daily life. These could be decisions related to your education, career, hobbies, or personal well-being. Practice making these choices mindfully, recognizing the role of independence in shaping your experiences and aspirations.

Joy

Discovering activities that filled me with joy was a turning point. I realized that by prioritizing joy, I was nourishing my spirit and empowering myself to face life's challenges with a renewed perspective.

Joy is the radiant energy that flows from engaging in activities that bring happiness, fulfillment, and a sense of purpose. For individuals with disabilities, cultivating joy is a transformative practice that enhances overall well-being and enriches the journey of empowerment. It's about embracing experiences that ignite passion and ignite a deep sense of contentment.

Joy is not a fleeting emotion—it's a state of being that emerges when you engage in activities that resonate with your interests and values. Whether it's pursuing a creative hobby, spending time with loved ones, or immersing yourself in nature, joy is a reminder of the beauty and abundance that life has to offer.

Cultivating joy involves embracing the present moment, even in the midst of challenges. By savoring the positive experiences and finding delight in the little things, individuals with disabilities can create a reservoir of positivity that fuels their resilience and sense of empowerment.

Engaging in activities that bring joy isn't just a luxury; it's a crucial aspect of mental and emotional health. Joy rejuvenates the spirit and enhances our capacity to navigate challenges.

Reflection:

Reflect on moments when you experienced profound joy in your life. What were you doing, and how did it make you feel? Consider how these moments of joy have impacted your overall well-being and outlook. Write down your reflections to remind yourself of the significance of cultivating joy.

Journal Entry:

Write about an activity or experience that consistently brings you joy. How does engaging in this activity enhance your sense of fulfillment and positivity? Reflect on how you can incorporate more of these joyful experiences into your daily life.

____

____

____

____

____

____

____

____

____

____

____

____

____

____

____

____

Activity:

Create a "Joy List" of activities that consistently bring you happiness. Include a variety of options, from simple pleasures to more elaborate pursuits. Whenever you're in need of a mood boost, consult your Joy List and engage in an activity that resonates with you in the moment.

Knowledge

The more I learned about accessible technology and resources, the more I realized the potential to create a more inclusive world. Knowledge gave me the tools to advocate for change.

Knowledge is the key that unlocks the doors to empowerment and informed decision-making. For individuals with disabilities, seeking knowledge is an empowering endeavor that equips them with the information and skills needed to navigate life's challenges and opportunities. It's about understanding their rights, options, and resources to make informed choices.

Knowledge empowers individuals to advocate for themselves and actively participate in decisions that affect their lives. By staying informed about the latest advancements in technology, accessible services, and relevant policies, individuals with disabilities can create pathways to success that align with their unique needs and aspirations.

Cultivating knowledge involves a commitment to lifelong learning. It's about embracing curiosity, seeking out new information, and recognizing that knowledge is a valuable asset that enriches every aspect of life.

Knowledge is a tool for empowerment, by understanding their rights and opportunities, individuals with disabilities can break down barriers and pave the way for greater inclusivity.

Reflection:

Reflect on a situation where seeking knowledge helped you make a more informed decision. How did your understanding of the situation change as a result of gaining knowledge? Consider the ways in which knowledge has played a role in your journey of empowerment. Write down your reflections to remind yourself of the power of knowledge.

Journal Entry:

Write about a topic or area of interest related to your disability that you're curious to learn more about. How might gaining knowledge in this area contribute to your personal growth and empowerment? Reflect on how you can incorporate opportunities for learning into your routine.

____

____

____

____

____

____

____

____

____

____

____

____

____

____

____

____

Activity:

Choose a subject related to disability rights, accessibility, or personal development that you're interested in learning more about. Research online resources, articles, or books that provide in-depth information on the topic. Dedicate time each week to learn and absorb new knowledge, recognizing the impact it can have on your journey of empowerment.

Love

Love isn't just an emotion; it's a force that fuels our resilience and empowers us to overcome obstacles. By surrounding ourselves with love, we tap into a wellspring of inner strength.

Love is the thread that weaves together the fabric of human connection and belonging. For individuals with disabilities, love is a source of strength, support, and resilience. It's about nurturing relationships that uplift the spirit and remind them of their inherent worth.

Love begins with self-love—a deep appreciation and acceptance of oneself, regardless of disability or challenges. It's about recognizing your own value and treating yourself with kindness and compassion. By cultivating self-love, individuals with disabilities can build a strong foundation of confidence and self-assurance.

Love also extends to the relationships with family, friends, and allies. These connections provide a network of support, encouragement, and understanding. By fostering loving relationships, individuals with disabilities create a sense of belonging and community that contributes to their overall well-being and empowerment.

Love is a powerful source of emotional nourishment. By cultivating self-love and nurturing positive relationships, individuals with disabilities can create a reservoir of strength that sustains them through challenges.

Reflection:

Reflect on moments when love—either self-love or love from others—has played a role in your journey of empowerment. How have loving relationships supported you during challenging times? Consider the ways in which love has contributed to your overall well-being and sense of belonging. Write down your reflections to remind yourself of the transformative power of love.

Journal Entry:

Write about a person or relationship that has had a positive impact on your life. How has the presence of love in this relationship influenced your sense of empowerment? Reflect on the ways in which love has shaped your journey and consider how you can nurture and strengthen loving connections.

____

____

____

____

____

____

____

____

____

____

____

____

____

____

____

____

Activity:

Create a "Love Letter" to yourself. Write a heartfelt letter that expresses your self-love and appreciation. Acknowledge your strengths, accomplishments, and the unique qualities that make you who you are. Whenever you need a reminder of your worth, read the love letter to yourself as an affirmation of your empowerment journey.

Mindfulness

Mindfulness helped me navigate the challenges of disability with grace. It allowed me to find moments of calm and clarity, even in the midst of uncertainty.

Mindfulness is the practice of being fully present in the moment, cultivating awareness of your thoughts, emotions, and surroundings. For individuals with disabilities, mindfulness is a powerful tool that enhances self-awareness, reduces stress, and fosters a deeper connection with the world around them. It's about embracing the present moment and finding calm amidst the chaos.

Mindfulness involves tuning into your senses and observing your thoughts without judgment. It's about letting go of worries about the past or anxieties about the future, and focusing on the here and now. By cultivating mindfulness, individuals with disabilities can create a space of peace and serenity within themselves.

Mindfulness also extends to self-compassion—a practice of treating oneself with kindness and understanding, especially in moments of difficulty. By practicing self-compassion, individuals with disabilities can nurture their emotional well-being and develop a more resilient mindset.

Mindfulness is a doorway to inner peace and self-discovery. By grounding ourselves in the present moment, we cultivate resilience and a greater sense of control over our emotions.

Reflection:

Reflect on a time when you practiced mindfulness and how it affected your well-being. How did being present in the moment influence your thoughts and emotions? Consider the ways in which mindfulness has contributed to your ability to navigate challenges with greater resilience. Write down your reflections to remind yourself of the power of mindfulness.

Journal Entry:

Write about a situation where practicing mindfulness helped you manage stress or anxiety. How did the practice of being present in the moment contribute to your emotional well-being? Reflect on how you can incorporate mindfulness into your daily routine to support your journey of empowerment.

____

____

____

____

____

____

____

____

____

____

____

____

____

____

____

____

Activity:

Engage in a mindfulness exercise. Find a quiet space and take a few minutes to focus on your breath. Notice the sensation of each inhale and exhale, bringing your attention back whenever your mind starts to wander. As you practice mindfulness, reflect on the sense of calm and clarity it brings to your mind and body.

Never Giving Up

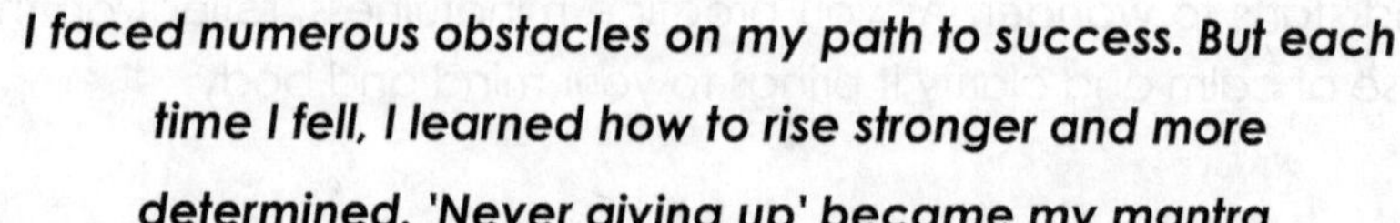

I faced numerous obstacles on my path to success. But each time I fell, I learned how to rise stronger and more determined. 'Never giving up' became my mantra.

"Never giving up" is the steadfast commitment to persevere in the face of challenges, setbacks, and obstacles. For individuals with disabilities, this determination is a cornerstone of empowerment. It's the refusal to be defined by limitations and the unwavering belief that with each hurdle, there's an opportunity to learn, grow, and ultimately succeed.

"Never giving up" involves resilience—the ability to bounce back from adversity and maintain a sense of determination. It's about acknowledging that failures are stepping stones on the path to success. By embracing this mindset, individuals with disabilities can navigate difficulties with grace and emerge stronger on the other side.

"Never giving up" also involves resilience—the ability to bounce back from adversity and maintain a sense of determination. It's about acknowledging that failures are stepping stones on the path to success. By embracing this mindset, individuals with disabilities can navigate difficulties with grace and emerge stronger on the other side.

Resilience is the heart of empowerment. It's the commitment to keep moving forward, no matter the challenges we face.

Reflection:

Reflect on a time when you embodied the spirit of "never giving up." How did your determination influence your approach to challenges? Consider the ways in which your resilience has shaped your sense of empowerment. Write down your reflections to remind yourself of the transformative power of perseverance.

Journal Entry:

Write about a goal or dream that you're determined to achieve. How does the mindset of "never giving up" play a role in your pursuit of this goal? Reflect on the steps you've taken to overcome obstacles and the lessons you've learned along the way.

____

____

____

____

____

____

____

____

____

____

____

____

____

____

____

____

Activity:

Create a visual representation of "never giving up" through art or collage. Use images, words, and symbols that capture the essence of determination and resilience. Display this visual reminder in a prominent place to inspire you on your journey of empowerment.

Overcoming Challenges

Each obstacle I encountered taught me valuable lessons. I learned that with the right mindset and support, no challenge is insurmountable.

Overcoming challenges is the embodiment of resilience, determination, and the refusal to be defined by obstacles. For individuals with disabilities, overcoming challenges is a testament to their strength, adaptability, and capacity to transform adversity into triumph. It's about facing difficulties head-on and using them as stepping stones towards personal growth.

Overcoming challenges involves embracing a growth mindset—the belief that skills and abilities can be developed through effort and perseverance. It's about viewing setbacks as opportunities to learn, evolve, and refine your strategies. By adopting this mindset, individuals with disabilities can approach challenges with confidence and curiosity.

Overcoming challenges also involves seeking support when needed. It's about recognizing that asking for help is a sign of strength, not weakness. By building a network of allies, individuals with disabilities can leverage collective wisdom and resources to tackle challenges more effectively.

Every challenge we face is an opportunity for growth. Individuals with disabilities who embrace challenges with determination are not only transforming their own lives but also inspiring others.

Reflection:

Reflect on a significant challenge you've overcome in your life. How did you approach the situation, and what strategies did you employ? Consider the lessons you learned from this experience and how it contributed to your personal growth and empowerment. Write down your reflections to remind yourself of the strength you possess.

Journal Entry:

Write about a recent challenge you're currently facing. How can you apply the lessons you've learned from past challenges to navigate this situation? Reflect on the support systems you have in place and the strategies you can use to overcome this obstacle.

Activity:

Engage in a role-playing activity where you imagine yourself successfully overcoming a specific challenge. Visualize the steps you would take, the strategies you would use, and the support you would seek. This exercise allows you to tap into your inner strength and build confidence in your ability to navigate challenges.

Perseverance

I encountered numerous roadblocks on my path. But I never lost sight of my goals. Perseverance allowed me to prove that my disability didn't define my potential.

Perseverance is the steadfast commitment to continue pursuing your goals and dreams, even in the face of adversity, setbacks, and obstacles. For individuals with disabilities, perseverance is a guiding light that illuminates the path to success. It's about staying resolute in your determination and maintaining a sense of purpose, no matter the challenges that arise.

Perseverance involves resilience—the ability to bounce back from failures and setbacks. It's about recognizing that setbacks are not the end of the journey but rather opportunities to learn, adapt, and grow. By embracing perseverance, individuals with disabilities can cultivate a resilient mindset that propels them forward.

Perseverance also involves tenacity—the willingness to put in the effort and work hard, even when progress is slow or obstacles seem insurmountable. It's about harnessing your inner strength and pushing through barriers with unwavering determination.

Perseverance is the foundation of achievement. Individuals with disabilities who persist in the face of challenges demonstrate an incredible capacity for growth and success.

Reflection:

Reflect on a time when you embodied the spirit of perseverance. How did your determination to continue moving forward influence the outcome? Consider the ways in which perseverance has shaped your journey of empowerment. Write down your reflections to remind yourself of the transformative power of tenacity.

Journal Entry:

Write about a long-term goal you've been working towards. How has your perseverance played a role in your progress? Reflect on the strategies you've used to stay committed and overcome challenges. Consider the small victories along the way and how they've contributed to your sense of achievement.

____

____

____

____

____

____

____

____

____

____

____

____

____

____

____

____

Activity:

Create a visual representation of perseverance through art or collage. Use images, words, and symbols that capture the essence of determination and resilience. Display this visual reminder in a prominent place to inspire you on your journey of empowerment.

Quality of Life

By focusing on my well-being and pursuing activities that bring joy, I've transformed my outlook. Quality of life isn't just about existing; it's about truly living.

Quality of life is the measure of overall well-being, happiness, and satisfaction in one's life. For individuals with disabilities, enhancing their quality of life is a fundamental goal. It's about creating a life that aligns with their values, aspirations, and unique needs, and finding ways to thrive despite challenges.

Quality of life involves holistic well-being—addressing physical, emotional, social, and psychological aspects. It's about prioritizing self-care, managing stress, and nurturing positive relationships. By tending to these various dimensions of well-being, individuals with disabilities can create a fulfilling and balanced life.

Quality of life also involves pursuing meaningful experiences and opportunities. It's about engaging in activities that bring joy, pursuing passions, and contributing to one's community. By embracing these opportunities, individuals with disabilities can shape a life that is rich in purpose and fulfillment.

Enhancing quality of life involves recognizing one's inherent worth and embracing the power to shape one's experiences. Individuals with disabilities who prioritize well-being are forging a path to empowerment.

Reflection:

Reflect on moments when you felt a high quality of life despite challenges. What factors contributed to your well-being and satisfaction? Consider the ways in which you've nurtured your holistic well-being and the impact it has had on your journey of empowerment. Write down your reflections to remind yourself of the importance of quality of life.

Journal Entry:

Write about an activity or experience that significantly enhances your quality of life. How does engaging in this activity contribute to your overall well-being and sense of fulfillment? Reflect on how you can continue to prioritize meaningful experiences in your life.

___

___

___

___

___

___

___

___

___

___

___

___

___

___

___

___

Activity:

Create a "Quality of Life Vision Board" that represents the various dimensions of well-being and fulfillment. Use images, words, and symbols that capture your aspirations for physical health, emotional well-being, relationships, and meaningful experiences. Display the vision board as a reminder of your commitment to enhancing your quality of life.

Resilience

Each challenge I faced was an opportunity to strengthen my resilience muscle. Resilience taught me that setbacks are not the end; they're the beginning of a new chapter.

Resilience is the inner strength that empowers individuals to navigate challenges, setbacks, and adversity with courage and determination. For individuals with disabilities, resilience is a cornerstone of empowerment—it's the capacity to rise above difficulties and thrive in the face of adversity. It's about bouncing back stronger, learning from experiences, and embracing the journey with unwavering determination.

Resilience involves adaptability—the ability to adjust to changing circumstances and find innovative solutions. It's about viewing challenges as opportunities for growth and transformation. By cultivating resilience, individuals with disabilities can harness their inner strength and weather the storms of life with grace.

Resilience also involves self-care—the practice of nurturing one's physical, emotional, and mental well-being. It's about recognizing when to rest, seeking support, and prioritizing activities that replenish the spirit. By taking care of themselves, individuals with disabilities can build a strong foundation of resilience that sustains them through challenges.

Resilience is the foundation of empowerment. By developing the capacity to bounce back from adversity, individuals with disabilities create a path to a more resilient future.

Reflection:

Reflect on a time when your resilience carried you through a difficult situation. How did your ability to bounce back influence the outcome? Consider the ways in which resilience has shaped your sense of empowerment and personal growth. Write down your reflections to remind yourself of the transformative power of resilience.

Journal Entry:

Write about a recent challenge you've faced and how your resilience helped you navigate it. Reflect on the strategies you employed to bounce back and how you learned from the experience. Consider the ways in which resilience contributes to your ability to thrive.

____

____

____

____

____

____

____

____

____

____

____

____

____

____

____

____

Activity:

Create a "Resilience Toolbox" by compiling a list of strategies that help you cultivate resilience. These could include self-care practices, mindfulness exercises, seeking support from loved ones, and engaging in activities that bring joy. Whenever you encounter a challenge, refer to your Resilience Toolbox to draw upon the resources that empower you to overcome obstacles.

Self-Advocacy

I learned that my voice has the power to create change. By speaking up and advocating for my needs, I'm contributing to a more inclusive world.

Self-advocacy is the act of speaking up for your own needs, rights, and preferences. For individuals with disabilities, self-advocacy is a crucial skill that empowers them to navigate the world with agency and assert their individuality. It's about recognizing that your voice matters and advocating for the accommodations and support you require.

Self-advocacy involves understanding your rights and responsibilities, particularly within the context of disability rights and accessibility. It's about communicating your needs effectively and working collaboratively with others to ensure your rights are upheld. By mastering the art of self-advocacy, individuals with disabilities can create a more inclusive and accessible world.

Self-advocacy also extends to challenging stereotypes and misconceptions about disabilities. It's about educating others and advocating for greater awareness and understanding. By sharing their stories and experiences, individuals with disabilities can promote positive change and foster a more inclusive society.

Self-advocacy is a cornerstone of empowerment. Individuals with disabilities who assert their needs and rights are not only advocating for themselves, but also for future generations.

Reflection:

Reflect on a situation where you practiced self-advocacy and how it influenced the outcome. How did advocating for your needs and rights empower you? Consider the ways in which self-advocacy has contributed to your journey of empowerment and the broader impact it can have.

Journal Entry:

Write about a time when you advocated for your needs or rights. How did you approach the situation, and what strategies did you use to communicate effectively? Reflect on the emotions and insights that arose from this experience.

___

___

___

___

___

___

___

___

___

___

___

___

___

___

___

___

Activity:

Engage in a role-playing activity where you practice self-advocacy in a hypothetical scenario. Imagine a situation where you need to communicate your needs or request accommodations. Practice using assertive communication and advocating for your rights. This exercise will help you build confidence in your ability to advocate for yourself in real-life situations.

Transformation

Every challenge I faced became an opportunity for transformation. I learned that by embracing change and remaining true to myself, I could create a life that exceeded my expectations.

Transformation is the profound process of evolving, growing, and becoming a stronger, more empowered version of oneself. For individuals with disabilities, transformation is a testament to their resilience, determination, and the ability to overcome challenges with grace. It's about embracing change as a catalyst for personal growth and empowerment.

Transformation involves a shift in mindset—the willingness to see challenges as opportunities and setbacks as stepping stones. It's about reframing difficulties as lessons that contribute to your journey. By adopting this transformative mindset, individuals with disabilities can harness their inner strength and forge a path of empowerment.

Transformation also involves embracing your unique identity—recognizing that your disability is just one aspect of who you are. It's about celebrating your strengths, passions, and achievements, and refusing to be defined solely by limitations. By embracing your whole self, you can embark on a journey of holistic transformation.

Transformation is the alchemy of empowerment. Individuals with disabilities who embrace change and growth are not only rewriting their narratives but also inspiring others to do the same.

Reflection:

Reflect on a moment of transformation in your life. How did facing challenges and embracing change contribute to your personal growth? Consider the ways in which transformation has influenced your journey of empowerment and the person you've become today. Write down your reflections to remind yourself of the power of growth and change.

Journal Entry:

Write about a specific area of your life where you're seeking transformation. How can you embrace change and challenges to create a positive shift? Reflect on the steps you can take to initiate transformation and the mindset you need to cultivate.

Activity:

Engage in a creative activity that symbolizes transformation, such as drawing, painting, or crafting. Capture the essence of growth and change through your chosen medium. Display your creation as a visual reminder of the transformative journey you're on.

Understanding

By engaging in open conversations and educating others, I've seen the impact of empathy and awareness. Understanding is the bridge to a more inclusive world.

Understanding is the bridge that connects individuals with disabilities to a world that may be unfamiliar or lacking in awareness. For individuals with disabilities, fostering understanding is a powerful step towards inclusion, empathy, and a more compassionate society. It's about creating opportunities for open dialogue, education, and dispelling misconceptions.

Understanding involves education—raising awareness about different types of disabilities, accessibility, and the challenges individuals may face. It's about promoting empathy and encouraging people to look beyond the surface to understand the lived experiences of those with disabilities. By fostering understanding, individuals with disabilities can pave the way for greater inclusivity.

Understanding also involves self-awareness—reflecting on one's own biases and assumptions and actively seeking to learn more. It's about recognizing the value of diversity and making an effort to create spaces that embrace and celebrate all individuals, regardless of their abilities.

Creating a more inclusive society starts with understanding. Individuals with disabilities who share their stories and educate others are contributing to a world where everyone is valued and respected.

Reflection:

Reflect on a time when someone took the time to understand your perspective or challenges. How did their effort to understand impact your sense of belonging and validation? Consider the ways in which fostering understanding has contributed to your journey of empowerment.

Journal Entry:

Write about a topic related to disability that you would like others to understand better. How can you communicate this topic in a way that fosters empathy and awareness? Reflect on the conversations and actions you can initiate to promote understanding.

____

Activity:

Engage in an educational initiative to foster understanding. This could involve giving a presentation, writing an article, or hosting a discussion about disability-related topics. By sharing your insights and experiences, you can contribute to creating a more informed and inclusive community.

Vision

My vision gave me purpose and direction. By believing in my abilities and setting intentions, I've achieved goals that once seemed impossible.

Vision is the driving force that propels individuals with disabilities towards their goals and aspirations. It's the ability to imagine a better future and take deliberate steps to make that vision a reality. For individuals with disabilities, cultivating a clear vision is a powerful tool for empowerment—it's about setting intentions and creating a roadmap for success.

Vision involves setting meaningful goals—identifying what you want to achieve and creating a plan to get there. It's about breaking down your aspirations into actionable steps and celebrating the progress along the way. By setting and pursuing goals, individuals with disabilities can shape their own narratives and create a life aligned with their vision.

Vision also involves self-belief—the confidence that you have what it takes to achieve your goals. It's about recognizing your strengths and capabilities and trusting in your ability to overcome challenges. By cultivating self-belief, individuals with disabilities can overcome self-doubt and move forward with determination.

A clear vision fuels motivation and direction. Individuals with disabilities who set meaningful goals and work towards them are empowering themselves to create the future they desire.

Reflection:

Reflect on a goal you've achieved or are currently working towards. How did your vision guide your actions and decisions? Consider the role of self-belief in your journey and the impact of setting meaningful goals on your sense of empowerment.

Journal Entry:

Write about a long-term vision you have for your future. How does this vision align with your values and aspirations? Reflect on the steps you can take to turn this vision into reality, and how each small action contributes to the bigger picture.

____

____

____

____

____

____

____

____

____

____

____

____

____

____

____

____

Activity:

Create a vision board that visually represents your goals and aspirations. Include images, quotes, and symbols that capture the essence of your vision. Display the vision board in a place where you'll see it daily, using it as a source of inspiration and motivation to stay aligned with your vision.

Wellness

Taking care of my well-being became my top priority. By recognizing my needs and seeking support, when necessary, I've been able to face challenges with a clear mind and open heart.

Wellness is the state of optimal physical, mental, and emotional well-being. For individuals with disabilities, prioritizing wellness is an essential component of empowerment. It's about recognizing that taking care of oneself holistically contributes to a fulfilling and empowered life.

Wellness involves self-care—the practice of engaging in activities that nourish your body, mind, and spirit. It's about recognizing your needs and making intentional choices to support your well-being. By prioritizing self-care, individuals with disabilities can build resilience, manage stress, and enhance their overall quality of life.

Wellness also involves seeking support—knowing when to reach out for assistance, whether it's from healthcare professionals, therapists, or support groups. It's about recognizing that seeking help is a sign of strength, not weakness. By embracing a support network, individuals with disabilities can navigate challenges with greater ease.

Wellness is the foundation of empowerment. Individuals with disabilities who prioritize their physical, mental, and emotional health are setting the stage for a life of fulfillment.

Reflection:

Reflect on a time when you prioritized your wellness and the impact it had on your overall well-being. How did engaging in self-care or seeking support contribute to your sense of empowerment? Consider the ways in which wellness has shaped your journey and your capacity to face challenges.

Journal Entry:

Write about a self-care practice that consistently supports your well-being. How does engaging in this practice enhance your physical, mental, or emotional health? Reflect on how you can continue to prioritize wellness in your daily life.

____

____

____

____

____

____

____

____

____

____

____

____

____

____

____

____

Activity:

Create a "Wellness Plan" that outlines specific self-care practices you will engage in regularly. Include physical, mental, and emotional well-being activities. Commit to prioritizing these practices and tracking your progress to ensure that you're nurturing your holistic wellness.

Xenodochia (Hospitable)

Taking care of my well-being became my top priority. By recognizing my needs and seeking support, when necessary, I've been able to face challenges with a clear mind and open heart.

Xenodochial is an uncommon term that means "hospitable" or "friendly to strangers." In the context of individuals with disabilities, fostering a xenodochial environment is about creating inclusive spaces where everyone feels welcome and valued. It's about recognizing the importance of empathy and kindness in promoting a more inclusive and supportive society.

Xenodochial environments involve cultivating empathy—putting yourself in others' shoes and seeking to understand their experiences and perspectives. It's about recognizing the uniqueness of each individual and valuing their contributions. By practicing empathy, individuals with disabilities can promote a culture of inclusivity.

Xenodochial environments also involve advocating for accessibility and inclusion. It's about recognizing that making spaces, services, and opportunities accessible benefits everyone. By advocating for inclusive practices, individuals with disabilities can help create a more xenodochial world where everyone can thrive.

Inclusive spaces benefit everyone. Individuals with disabilities who champion accessibility and empathy are fostering a more compassionate and welcoming society.

By advocating for accessible spaces and sharing my story, I've witnessed the positive impact of inclusivity. Xenodochial environments celebrate our shared humanity.

Reflection:

Reflect on a time when you experienced a xenodochial environment where you felt truly welcome and valued. How did this experience influence your sense of belonging and empowerment? Consider the ways in which promoting inclusivity and empathy has contributed to your journey.

Journal Entry:

Write about an instance where you took steps to create a more inclusive and xenodochial environment. How did you promote empathy, accessibility, or understanding? Reflect on the impact of these actions on yourself and those around you.

____

____

____

____

____

____

____

____

____

____

____

____

____

____

____

____

Activity:

Engage in a kindness challenge where you actively seek opportunities to create a xenodochial environment. Practice acts of kindness, empathy, and inclusivity throughout your day. Notice how these actions impact your own well-being and the well-being of those around you, and reflect on the ripple effect of your efforts.

Yearning for Change

I realized that I could be a force for change. By harnessing my yearning and taking action, I'm contributing to a world where everyone's voice is heard.

Yearning for change is the deep desire and aspiration for a better future—for oneself and for the world. For individuals with disabilities, this yearning is a driving force that propels them to advocate for their rights, challenge societal norms, and actively work towards a more inclusive and equitable society. It's about recognizing the need for change and taking meaningful action to make it a reality.

Yearning for change involves advocacy—using your voice and influence to raise awareness about important issues, challenge stereotypes, and demand equality. It's about recognizing that change is a collective effort and that every individual's contribution matters. By advocating for change, individuals with disabilities can be catalysts for progress.

Yearning for change also involves empowerment—recognizing your own agency and ability to shape the world around you. It's about believing in your capacity to create positive change and inspiring others to do the same. By embracing the yearning for change, individuals with disabilities can contribute to a more just and inclusive future.

Yearning for change is the heartbeat of empowerment. Individuals with disabilities who channel their yearning into advocacy are paving the way for a more inclusive and equitable world.

Reflection:

Reflect on the changes you yearn to see in the world—for yourself, your community, or society at large. How does your yearning for change influence your actions and decisions? Consider the ways in which your advocacy and empowerment contribute to the progress you envision.

Journal Entry:

Write about a specific change you are yearning for in relation to disability rights, accessibility, or inclusion. How can you use your voice and actions to advocate for this change? Reflect on the steps you can take to transform your yearning into meaningful impact.

Activity:

Engage in a reflective activity where you visualize the change you yearn to see. Close your eyes and imagine a future where this change has become a reality. Envision the positive impact it has on individuals with disabilities and society as a whole. Use this visualization as inspiration to continue advocating and working towards the change you yearn for.

Zeal for Life

My passions became my driving force. By embracing what brings me joy, I've discovered an unwavering source of empowerment.

Zeal for life is the enthusiasm, passion, and vibrant energy that infuses every aspect of one's existence. For individuals with disabilities, cultivating a zeal for life is a powerful act of empowerment. It's about embracing life's joys, pursuing passions, and creating a sense of purpose that transcends challenges.

Zeal for life involves embracing positivity—focusing on the bright side of things, finding joy in everyday moments, and cultivating an optimistic outlook. It's about recognizing that a positive mindset can transform how you experience the world. By fostering positivity, individuals with disabilities can elevate their overall well-being.

Zeal for life also involves pursuing passions—engaging in activities that bring immense joy and fulfillment. It's about pursuing hobbies, interests, and creative outlets that ignite your spirit and nourish your soul. By indulging in your passions, individuals with disabilities can infuse their lives with a sense of purpose and zest.

A zestful approach to life is a key to empowerment. Individuals with disabilities who radiate enthusiasm and positivity inspire those around them.

Reflection:

Reflect on the moments when you've felt a strong zeal for life, despite challenges. How did embracing positivity and pursuing passions contribute to your overall sense of empowerment? Consider the ways in which cultivating zeal for life has shaped your journey and mindset.

Journal Entry:

Write about an activity or hobby that fills you with zeal for life. How does engaging in this activity contribute to your overall well-being and sense of fulfillment? Reflect on how you can continue to prioritize these sources of joy in your life.

____

____

____

____

____

____

____

____

____

____

____

____

____

____

____

____

Activity:

Engage in a passion-driven project or activity that brings you immense joy. Dedicate time to pursuing your passion and immerse yourself in the experience. Notice how your enthusiasm and positivity are enhanced, and reflect on how this passion contributes to your overall empowerment.

Epilogue: A Journey of Empowerment

As we reach the end of this journey, let us reflect on the remarkable tapestry of empowerment woven by individuals with disabilities. The stories shared, insights gained, and actions taken have illuminated the path to a more inclusive, empathetic, and compassionate world. Each chapter of this book has showcased the power of resilience, the beauty of diversity, and the unwavering determination to rise above challenges.

The journey of empowerment is not linear, nor is it without its share of obstacles. Yet, the individuals who have contributed to these pages have demonstrated that even in the face of adversity, empowerment can be found. It is found in the acceptance of oneself, the embrace of change, the pursuit of dreams, and the advocacy for equal rights and understanding.

May these words serve as a reminder that empowerment is not confined to a singular moment—it is a continuous evolution, a transformation of the spirit, and an ongoing commitment to growth. The stories within these chapters remind us that empowerment is a collective effort, where every voice, every action, and every step taken contribute to a more just and inclusive world.

As we close this chapter, may the insights shared in this book serve as a wellspring of inspiration for each reader. May you carry forth the spirit of acceptance, resilience, self-advocacy, and compassion into your own lives and communities. And may you, too, become agents of change, advocates of understanding, and champions of empowerment for all.

The journey of empowerment is ongoing, and its impact is immeasurable. Let us continue to foster environments of inclusivity, embrace the power of diverse perspectives, and work together to create a world where every individual can thrive, regardless of their abilities.

With gratitude and hope for a brighter future,

Alexis JC

Acknowledgments

This book is the culmination of shared experiences, heartfelt stories, and the collective wisdom of many individuals who have contributed their insights, expertise, and voices. The journey of creating this book has been a collaborative effort, and I am deeply grateful to all those who have supported and inspired its creation.

I would like to express my sincere gratitude to the individuals with disabilities who generously shared their stories, reflections, and expertise. Your courage, resilience, and willingness to share your experiences have been the heart and soul of this book. Your voices have shed light on the diverse and powerful journey of empowerment.

I would also like to extend my appreciation to the experts and advocates who contributed their insights and wisdom to enrich the content of this book. Your expertise has added depth and authenticity to the chapters, providing readers with a comprehensive understanding of the topics explored.

I am thankful for the invaluable guidance and support provided by mentors, educators, and professionals who have helped shape the direction of this book. Your encouragement and feedback have been instrumental in its development.

I extend my thanks to my family, friends, and colleagues for their unwavering support and encouragement throughout this journey. Your belief in the importance of this project has been a driving force, and your words of encouragement have kept me motivated.

Lastly, I would like to express my gratitude to the readers of this book. Your openness to learning, your commitment to understanding, and your desire to create positive change in the world are what make this endeavor worthwhile.

Thank you to all who have played a part in bringing this book to life. Your contributions have made this journey of empowerment possible, and I am honored to have shared it with each and every one of you.

With heartfelt appreciation,

Alexis JC

About the Book

"Empowerment ABC: A Journey of Resilience for People with Disabilities" is a book that delves into the diverse and inspiring journeys of individuals with disabilities. Through a collection of thought-provoking chapters, personal stories, expert insights, and interactive activities, this book aims to illuminate the path to empowerment, shed light on the challenges faced, and celebrate the triumphs achieved.

With a focus on themes such as acceptance, advocacy, resilience, self-belief, and more, each chapter offers a deep exploration of the experiences and insights that shape the lives of individuals with disabilities. Through a participatory approach, readers are encouraged to reflect on their own journeys, write in journals, engage in activities, and draw inspiration from the profound stories shared within these pages.

" Empowerment ABC: A Journey of Resilience for People with Disabilities" goes beyond mere storytelling—it serves as a resource for those seeking to understand the experiences of individuals with disabilities, offering expert insights, actionable advice, and a roadmap for creating a more inclusive and compassionate society. From embracing change to fostering understanding, from self-advocacy to celebrating one's uniqueness, this book serves as a guide to empowerment for individuals of all abilities.

Whether you are an individual with a disability seeking inspiration and validation, a caregiver looking to better understand the experiences of your loved ones, an educator aiming to create inclusive spaces, or a curious reader seeking insights into the human spirit's resilience, " Empowerment ABC: A Journey of Resilience for People with Disabilities" invites you to embark on a transformative journey of self-discovery, empathy, and empowerment.

Join us in unraveling the stories that embody the power of the human spirit, and let " Empowerment ABC: A Journey of Resilience for People with Disabilities" inspire you to believe in the limitless potential that resides within us all.

About the Author

Alexis Jose Cabauatan, the author of "Empowerment ABC: A Journey of Resilience for People with Disabilities," is a prolific writer and passionate advocate hailing from the bustling city of Manila, Philippines. With a fervent dedication to empowering others and promoting positive change, Alexis's literary journey is marked by impactful storytelling that resonates with readers worldwide.

Alexis is also the visionary behind "Back on My Two Feet: A Life of an Amputee—Inspiring Resilience, Triumph, and the Power of the Human Spirit," a heartfelt memoir that chronicles their personal odyssey of overcoming adversity, discovering strength, and embracing a life brimming with possibilities after amputation. This memoir serves as a testament to Alexis's indomitable spirit and ability to conquer challenges with unwavering resilience.

Furthermore, Alexis authored "Beyond the Shadows: Conquering Overthinking and Embracing a Life of Empowerment," a book that offers readers invaluable insights, practical strategies, and personal anecdotes to navigate the labyrinth of overthinking and usher in a life infused with empowerment, clarity, and purpose.

As an author, Alexis firmly believes in the transformative influence of words and narratives. Driven by a desire to cultivate understanding, advocate for inclusivity, and ignite positive change, they consistently contribute to the literary realm with stories that motivate, enlighten, and elevate the human experience.

Through the medium of writing and advocacy, Alexis aspires to propagate waves of positivity, empathy, and empowerment, both locally and on a global scale. " Empowerment ABC: A Journey of Resilience for People with Disabilities " exemplifies their commitment to amplifying the voices and stories of individuals with disabilities, nurturing comprehension, and cultivating a more inclusive and compassionate world.

Stay connected with Alexis Jose Cabauatan on their social media platforms and follow their journey as an author, advocate, and catalyst for transformation.

For inquiries, speaking engagements, or collaboration opportunities, please reach out to phScriber@gmail.com.

Alexis Jose Cabauatan

Author of "Empowerment ABC: A Journey of Resilience for People with Disabilities"

Empowerment ABC:

A Journey of Resilience for People with Disabilities

1st edition

September 2023

Published by:

ALEXIS JOSE CABAUATAN
scriberPH
Manila, Philippines
alexis.j.cabauatan@gmail.com

+63 995 247 1322
+63 918 398 7461